Grades K-4

FOCUS ON ELEMENTARY PHYSICS

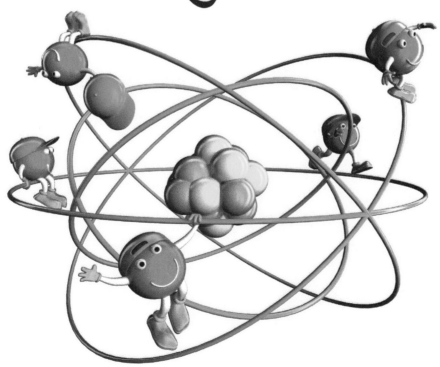

Rebecca W. Keller, PhD

Text illustrations: Janet Moneymaker, Rebecca W. Keller, PhD

Focus On Elementary Physics Student Textbook (hardcover)
ISBN 978-1-936114-75-7

Published by Gravitas Publications, Inc.
www.gravitaspublications.com

GRAVITAS
PUBLICATIONS

iv Contents

Chapter 1 What Is Physics?

1.1 What Goes Up Comes Down

Have you ever thrown a ball up in the air? Did you notice the ball when it left your hand? What did it do? Did it go up? Did it come back down? Unless it gets stuck in a tree or picked up by a big bird, a ball that is thrown up into the air will always come back down.

Have you ever tried to throw a ball really far or really high? Have you ever watched how far or how high the ball goes? Have you ever noticed that it's harder to throw a heavy ball than it is to throw a light ball? Have you ever noticed that it's almost impossible to throw a feather?

All of these questions are questions about physics. Physics is the branch of science that asks questions about how far or how high a ball might go or how heavy it needs to be so that it can be thrown. People who study physics are studying how the world works.

1.2 Obey the Rules

Did you know that balls will follow the same rules no matter where you are on Earth? You

can be in the frozen arctic, and if you drop two balls they will fall in exactly the same way. You can be in a desert or at the beach or on a boat, and if you drop two balls, they will fall in exactly the same way. No matter where you are on the Earth, a ball will always follow the rules.

There are rules for the way things, like balls, behave. The rule "what goes up comes down" is a rule about gravity. Gravity is what makes the ball come back down. Gravity is also what keeps you from flying off the surface of the Earth. Balls, toys, cars, houses, even birds, obey the rules of gravity.

1.3 Who Makes the Rules?

Physics is about studying the way things behave and then figuring out the rules. Today, scientists who study physics are called physicists. Physicists don't make the rules, but they discover the rules by watching how the world works. Galileo Galilei was an Italian astronomer who liked to watch the sky. But Galileo was also curious about

how things moved. He is known for a famous experiment in which he dropped two balls off a building to see what would happen. He used a heavy ball and a light ball, and he found out that they both hit the ground at the same time!

Physicists also use math to figure out the rules. Isaac Newton was a great scientist who used math to figure out many important rules. Just by using math, Newton figured out exactly why Galileo's balls hit the ground at the same time when dropped off a building. Math helps us understand the rules.

1.4 Think Like a Scientist

The first thing scientists do is to make observations. When you are looking at something with your eyes, you are making an observation. Making good observations is the first and most important step when you are trying to think like a scientist.

When you make an observation, try to notice everything you can about what you are observing. If you are at the movie theater getting popcorn, try to notice the popcorn machine. Where does the popcorn go in?

Where does it come out? What is moving on the machine? What is staying still? Notice the popcorn when it comes out. Is it hot or is it cold? These are important observations if you want to think like a scientist.

1.5 Summary

- Objects, like balls and planes and birds, always obey the rules of physics.

- The rules of physics are true no matter where you are on the Earth.

- Physicists don't make the rules, they discover the rules.

- To think like a scientist, you must make good observations.

Chapter 2 Push and Pull

2.1 Up the Hill

What do you think would happen if you tried to take your baby sister up a hill in a wagon? At first you might grab the handle of the wagon, and as you do, you might feel the wagon pull against you.

You might think that the wagon with your sister in it is heavy. To get the wagon moving by pulling on it, you might need to use all of the strength in your arms and legs. Once the wagon is moving, you might find that it is easy to roll your sister along the road and that you don't have to use as many muscles. But, as you get to the bottom of the hill, you might need to use all your muscles again to pull the wagon uphill. When you reach the top of the hill, you might discover that you are completely out of breath and a little tired. You might say that you used all your energy to do the work you needed to do to get your sister up the hill. And a physicist would say you are exactly right!

When you pull your little sister up a hill in a wagon, you are doing work and you are using energy. In physics, work is what happens when force moves an object. Energy gives you the ability to do work. But what is force? And what is energy?

2.2 Force

When you are pulling the wagon up the hill, you are using a force. Force is any action that changes the location of an object. Because you are changing the location of the wagon (and your sister), you are using force.

Force is also any action that changes the shape of an object. If you were to squeeze a marshmallow, you would be using force. By squeezing a marshmallow you are changing its shape with the force created by your hands.

Force is also any action that changes how fast or how slow an object is moving. You may have experienced this kind of force if you ever tried to catch the same ball as your friend. If you were both looking at the ball and not where you were going, you might have run into each other. When that happens—WHAM!—the two of you collide, and you both stop moving. In this action you each used force to stop the other from moving. You could probably feel the effects of the force stay with your head or knees for several hours!

Force is any action that changes the location of an object or the shape of an object or how fast or slowly an object is moving.

2.3 Work

In the first section we saw that work happens when force moves an object. Work also happens when force changes the shape of an object or when force changes how fast or how slowly an object is moving.

How is work related to force? If you use more force are you doing more work? Maybe. Or if you are doing more work, are you using more force? Yes!

Imagine that instead of one little sister, you have two. And imagine trying to pull both little sisters up the hill in the wagon. It will take more muscles, more energy, and more effort to move two little sisters up the hill. In fact, if your little sisters were twins and weighed exactly the same, you would have to do twice the amount of work to get both of them up the hill.

The same is true for squeezing a marshmallow or running into your friend. If you squeeze the marshmallow more, you are doing more work. If you and your friend are running faster, generating more force, you are doing more work when you run into each other.

2.4 Energy

How do you get the energy for pulling your sisters up the hill in a wagon or for squeezing a marshmallow or for colliding with your friend?

Where does the energy come from? The energy for you to do all these things comes from your breakfast. When you eat breakfast, you are giving

your body the energy it needs to do work. In physics, energy is something that gives something else the ability to do work. When you eat eggs or toast or cereal, your body takes the energy in the food and uses it in a way that helps your muscles move. The food you eat for breakfast gives your muscles the ability to do work—like pulling a wagon full of sisters up a hill! And that's a lot of work.

2.5 Summary

- Work is what happens when a force moves an object.

- A force is any action that changes the location of an object or the shape of an object or how fast or slowly an object is moving.

- Energy is something that gives something else the ability to do work.

Chapter 3 Kinds of Energy

3.1 Stored Energy

Recall from Chapter 2 that energy is something that gives something else the ability to do work. We saw how the food you eat for breakfast gives you the ability to move your muscles which allows you to pull your little sister up a hill.

The food you eat for breakfast is a type of stored energy. Stored energy is energy that has not been used. A box of cereal may not look like it is full of energy, but in fact it has lots of energy molecules.

These energy molecules are called carbohydrates. When your body needs energy, it will break down the carbohydrate molecules so they can be used for moving muscles or walking to the store.

3.2 Types of Stored Energy

There are different types of stored energy. Have you ever taken a rubber band and stretched it across your finger and thumb? What happens when you release your thumb, letting the rubber band go? It flies through the air. There is stored energy in a rubber band.

But can you use this stored energy for breakfast? NO! You wouldn't eat rubber bands for breakfast!

A rubber band has a different type of stored energy than your breakfast cereal.

Breakfast cereal has chemical stored energy. Chemical stored energy is energy that comes from chemicals and chemical reactions. A rubber band has elastic stored energy.

Elastic stored energy is energy that is found in materials that can stretch. A book on a table has gravitational stored energy. It could do work if it were to fall to the ground and smash an egg. Gravitational stored energy comes from objects that are elevated above the ground and can be pulled down by gravity.

3.3 Releasing Stored Energy

When you let a rubber band go from your thumb, you release the stored elastic energy, and the rubber band flies through the air. When you eat cereal for breakfast, your body breaks down the carbohydrate molecules, releasing the stored chemical energy so your muscles can pull a wagon. If a book falls off a table and onto the floor, the stored gravitational energy of the book is released and can be used to break an egg.

When each of these types of stored energy is released, the energy does not disappear but is converted into moving energy. The rubber band moved, the wagon moved, and the book moved. In order for stored energy to do work, it must first be released. The stored energy in the rubber band, the breakfast cereal, and the book were all released and changed into moving energy. But what is moving energy?

3.4 Moving Energy

Moving energy is the energy found in moving objects. There is only one type of moving energy, and physicists call this energy kinetic energy. Kinetic energy can come from different types of stored energy, but only the energy of a moving object is called kinetic energy.

When you release the stored energy in a rubber band and it's sitting on the floor, it can no longer do any work unless it is picked up and stretched again. When the rubber band is sitting on the floor, all of the stored energy has been released, and all of the kinetic energy has been used. You might think that the energy is lost. However, none of the energy disappears, it just gets changed to a different type of energy. Energy is conserved. That means energy doesn't get lost, but it is changed from one form to another form. We will learn more about how energy is conserved in Chapter 10.

3.5 Summary

- Stored energy is energy that has not been used yet.

- There are different types of stored energy. Breakfast cereal has chemical stored energy. A rubber band has elastic stored energy.

- When stored energy is released, it can be changed into kinetic energy—the energy of an object that is moving.

Chapter 4 When Things Move

4.1 Moving Objects

In the last chapter we saw that stored energy can make an object move. We saw that when an object moves, stored energy is changed into kinetic energy. But once an object is moving, how does it keep moving?

We saw in Chapter 2 that work happens when a force moves an object. You might think that forces also keep objects moving. This is what Aristotle thought. Aristotle was a philosopher from Greece who studied how objects move. Aristotle thought that objects move because forces push

on them from behind. However, 2000 years later Galileo discovered that forces don't keep objects moving. Forces actually stop objects from moving. Forces can also change the direction of a moving object. But forces don't keep objects moving.

4.2 Keeping Objects in Motion

Galileo discovered that once an object is moving, it will keep moving unless it is stopped by a force. Forces can start an object moving or stop it, but forces do not keep an object moving. So, what keeps an object moving? An object keeps moving because of inertia. But what is inertia?

Have you ever been playing with your friends on the back porch when your mom called you to dinner? Maybe you didn't want to go to dinner. Maybe you wanted to keep playing. Maybe you  even refused to stop playing and didn't go to dinner. That is inertia.

Inertia is when an object resists a change in motion. When you kept playing with your friend and did not want to change what you were doing to go to dinner, you had inertia. You didn't want to change your motion (playing) to a new motion (going to dinner). When you resisted going to dinner, you were like an object that doesn't want to stop moving. That is inertia.

Inertia also keeps objects still. When an object is moving, it wants to stay moving, and when an object is still, it wants to stay still. When an object does not want to change from moving to still or from still to moving, we say it has inertia.

4.3 Marbles and Bowling Balls

Everything has inertia. Bananas, oranges, bowling balls and marbles all have inertia. You have inertia. If you are standing in the middle of your room refusing to put your pajamas on, that is inertia. If you are running down a hill and you can't stop, that is inertia. So whether you are moving or not moving, you have inertia. Whether you are tall or short, young or old, you have inertia. Everything that has mass has inertia. But what is mass?

In physics inertia comes from a property called mass. Everything has inertia because everything has mass. Simply put, on Earth mass is how heavy something is. A heavy bowling ball has more inertia than a light marble. Because a bowling ball weighs more (has more mass) than a marble, it has more inertia. Think about how hard it is to roll a bowling ball.

Now think about how easy it is to roll a marble. It is harder to get a bowling ball to move than it is to get a marble to move. Why? Because a bowling ball has more inertia. It is also harder to get a bowling ball to stop moving than it is to stop a marble. Why? Again, because a bowling ball has more inertia than a marble.

4.4 Friction

We said that objects don't stop moving unless a force makes them stop. Because everything has inertia, an object in motion will stay in motion.

But wait! If you roll a soccer ball on the soccer field, it will eventually stop even if another soccer player doesn't make it stop. Why? Why does a soccer ball stop moving even if no one is there to make it stop?

It stops moving because of friction. Remember, all objects will keep moving (because all objects have inertia) unless a force makes them stop moving. Everywhere on Earth, friction makes things stop moving. Friction is a force that stops objects from moving. Friction can come from almost anything. The grass in the soccer field makes friction that stops the rolling soccer ball. If a ball is thrown into a swimming pool, the ball will eventually stop moving because of the friction created by the water. Even air creates friction. If a ball is thrown into the sky, it will eventually slow down and stop moving because of friction caused by the air.

4.5 Summary

- Forces make objects start to move, and forces also stop objects from moving. But forces do not keep objects moving.

- Inertia keeps objects still and keeps objects moving.

- Friction is a force that will stop objects from moving.

Chapter 5 Chemical Energy

5.1 Atoms and Energy

In Chapter 4 you learned about mass and inertia. Every material object has mass. A tree has mass. A football has mass. You have mass. We also saw in Chapter 4 that the more mass an object has, the more inertia it has. That is, the more mass an object has, the harder it is to get the object moving or to get the object to stop moving.

Every material object has mass because every object is made of atoms. Atoms are what make objects into objects. A tree is made of atoms. A fish is made of atoms. Your body is made of atoms.

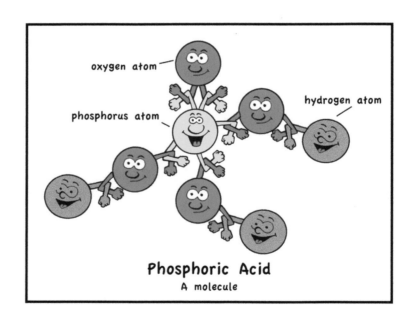

oxygen atom

hydrogen atom

phosphorus atom

Phosphoric Acid
A molecule

When two or more atoms are connected together, a molecule is formed. Phosphoric acid is a molecule made of the atoms oxygen, hydrogen and phosphorus.

When molecules interact with other molecules or atoms, a chemical reaction takes place.

What happens when you add baking soda to vinegar? Bubbles start to form, and the baking soda turns to foam. This is a chemical reaction. It takes energy for a chemical reaction to occur. Where did the baking soda and vinegar get the energy? The energy is inside the baking soda and vinegar molecules. This is called chemical energy. Remember in Chapter 3 we talked about stored energy. Atoms and molecules have stored chemical energy. When a chemical reaction occurs, the energy stored inside the molecules is released and used to do work.

You can see the work being done if you put baking soda and vinegar together in a bottle and close the lid. The stored chemical energy of the baking soda and vinegar in the bottle will release, causing a chemical reaction. The chemical reaction will make gas which will begin to press on the sides and top of the bottle and will put pressure on the lid. If there is enough energy used and enough gas created, the bottle might explode and the lid pop off! This is stored chemical energy being used to do work.

5.2 Energy for Cars

How does your car get energy for moving? Does your mom feed the car hamburgers? Or do your parents take it to a field and let it graze on the grass with the cows?

No! Your parents take your car to the gas station to fill the gas tank with gasoline.

Gasoline is a type of stored chemical energy used for fuel by cars, motorcycles, airplanes and boats. The stored chemical energy in gasoline is released when your mom or dad start the car. When the chemical energy is released, it can be used to move the parts of the car so that its wheels can roll down the street.

5.3 Energy in Food

In Chapter 3 we saw how the cereal you eat for food is a type of stored energy. Food, like potatoes, cereal, and bread, contain a type of stored chemical energy called carbohydrates.

Carbohydrates are special kinds of molecules that living things use for fuel. Sugar is a type of carbohydrate. Our bodies use lots of carbohydrates for energy.

The body breaks down carbohydrate molecules and uses the energy to move muscles, to make our heart beat, and even to think! It takes lots of energy to think, and eating carbohydrates is one way to give our bodies the fuel needed for thinking!

5.4 Batteries

Batteries are another type of stored chemical energy. What happens when you put batteries in a flashlight or in a game player? Inside a battery are metals and chemicals. When the metal and chemicals come in contact with each other, a chemical reaction occurs. The chemical energy inside the battery is changed into electrical energy, and the electrical energy runs the flashlight or game player. We'll learn more about electrical energy in Chapter 6.

5.5 Summary

- Chemical energy comes from atoms and molecules released in chemical reactions.

- Gasoline is a type of stored chemical energy used by cars, boats, and motorcycles.

- Carbohydrates are a type of stored chemical energy used by living things.

- Batteries are a type of stored chemical energy used by flashlights and game players.

Chapter 6   Electricity

6.1 Introduction

In Chapter 5 you learned about different types of chemical energy. Recall that chemical energy is energy inside atoms and molecules. When a chemical reaction occurs, chemical energy is released from the atoms and molecules. You also learned that sometimes chemical energy is converted into electrical energy. Batteries convert chemical energy into electrical energy. But exactly where does the electrical energy come from?

6.2 Electrons

Electricity or electrical energy comes from electrons. An electron is part of an atom.

Look at your body. Notice that your body has different parts. You have eyes for seeing, legs for walking, and arms for picking up objects. Inside your body you also have lots of parts. You have lungs for breathing, a stomach for digesting food, and a heart for pumping blood. You have many parts to your body, and each part does something different.

In a similar way, an atom has different parts. An atom has three main parts called protons, neutrons, and electrons. The protons and neutrons are in the center of the atom, and the electrons move around outside this center.

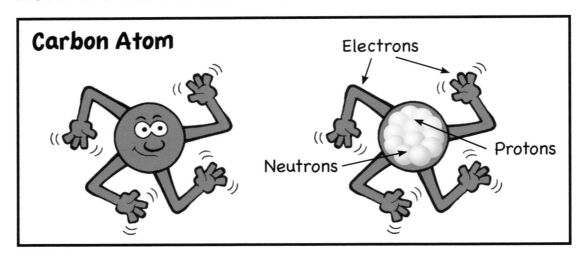

Carbon Atom

Electrons

Protons

Neutrons

The electrons are what make atoms stick to each other to form molecules during a chemical reaction. In the illustration, the electrons are shown as the "arms" on the carbon atom.

The electrons of an atom can jump back and forth during a chemical reaction. That is, atoms can exchange electrons. You can't give your arms to someone else when you meet them, but an atom can give part of itself (the electron) to another atom to form a chemical bond. It is the moving of these electrons that causes electrical energy. In a metal, lots of electrons jump from atom to atom all the time.

6.3 Electrons and Charge

What happens when you rub a balloon in your mom's hair? If you pull the balloon away just slightly, your mom's hair will travel with the balloon. Physicists say that the balloon is charged. In this case, "charged" means that the balloon is attracted to the hair and the hair is attracted to the balloon. But why? Why does the balloon attract your mom's hair and the hair attract the balloon? What makes the balloon "charged?"

Electrons make the balloon charged. Electrons have a charge. That means that they have the ability to attract or repel other things that also have a charge. Protons have a charge but neutrons are neutral. Neutrons have no charge (that is why they are called neutrons, because they are neutral). Physicists and chemists say that electrons are negatively charged and protons are positively charged. It is just one way to say that their charges are opposite. This is just a "rule" that scientists follow so it is easier to talk about charges.

In physics, opposites attract. Positive charges attract negative charges, and negative charges attract positive charges. So protons attract electrons, and electrons attract protons. When you rub the balloon in your mom's hair, electrons hop from your mom's hair to the balloon. Because there are now more electrons on the balloon, it is negatively charged. Your mom's hair lost some electrons, so it is positively charged. Because your mom's hair and the balloon are charged with opposite charges, they attract each other!

6.4 Electrons and Force

Remember from Chapter 2 that forces cause things to move. This is true for large things, like wagons, and small things, like electrons. Electrical forces cause electrons to move.

Have you ever rubbed your feet on the carpet and then touched a door knob? If the air was dry enough, you probably felt the effects of electrical forces moving electrons. You might have felt a small shock when —ZAP!— you touched the door knob. This is electrical force moving electrons.

6.5 Summary

- Electricity or electrical energy comes from electrons.

- Electrons are part of an atom. Atoms have protons, neutrons, and electrons.

- Electrons can move from atom to atom.

- Electrons are negatively charged. Protons are positively charged, and neutrons are neutral.

Chapter 7 Moving Electrons

7.1 Introduction

In Chapter 6 you learned how electrical energy comes from the movement of electrons. You learned that electrons can jump from atom to atom, or even from hair to balloons! You also learned that electrons are charged and that scientists say that electrons have a negative charge and protons have a positive charge.

Everything that is made of atoms has electrons. All material objects have electrons. Wooden tables have electrons. Marshmallows have electrons. Frogs have electrons.

Many kinds of materials will allow a small number of electrons to move through them. But only some types of materials allow lots of electrons to move through them. Scientists say that these types of materials conduct electricity. This means that lots of electrons can flow through them, like water flowing through a garden hose.

7.2 Electrons in Metals

If you look at the toaster, you notice that it is connected to a cable, and this cable is plugged into the wall. Inside the wall is another cable that goes outside and connects to a big pole. This pole has cables on it that bring electricity into your house. The toaster needs to be plugged into the wall to get electricity in order to work. This is also true for your computer (if it doesn't have a battery). It is also true for your television set or video game player. All of these items need electrical energy to work. And all of these items are connected to wires or cables that are plugged into the cable in the wall that

brings the electricity into your house.

If you open up one of the cables, you might see that it is made of metal wires. Copper metal is often at the center of most cables or wires because copper can conduct electricity. The reason copper can conduct electricity (allow electrons to flow) is because some of the electrons on the copper atoms are very loosely attached. That is, the electrons can easily jump from one atom to the next.

Copper atoms have lots of electrons. In the illustration the "arms" on each copper atom are replaced with dots to represent the electrons. In a piece of copper metal lots of copper atoms are next to each other. This means that there are lots of electrons free to hop around. This is why copper is a good conductor.

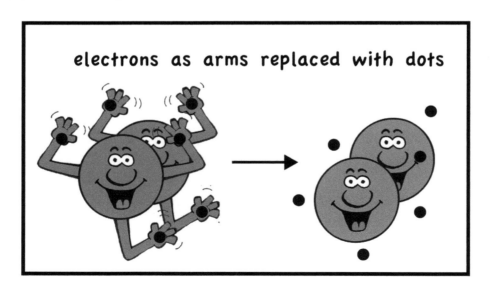

electrons as arms replaced with dots

Just like water can flow through a garden hose because the water molecules are not attached to the hose, electrons can flow through a metal wire because the electrons are not tightly attached to the metal atoms.

7.3 Electrons in Other Materials

You saw in the introduction that all materials have electrons. Marshmallows, teddy bears, wooden tables, and popcorn all have electrons. But these materials are not used for moving electrons. Scientists say that these materials do not conduct electricity. That is, they do not allow the electrons to hop from one atom to the next. The electrons in materials that do not conduct electricity are more tightly held to the atoms. Because they can't hop from atom to atom, there is no flow of electrons through the materials.

Scientists call these materials insulators. If you look closely at the cable that connects your toaster to the wall, you will see that it is covered in plastic. Plastic is an insulator. Plastic does not allow electrons to move through it, so it does not conduct electricity.

Insulators keep the electrons from moving from wires to your hands. This is important because even though you are not made of metal, your body will conduct electricity! If you touch a wire used for moving electricity and it does not have a plastic covering, you could get a big shock! This

is why it is always important to be careful not to touch electric wires or electric outlets. The amount of electricity that moves through the wires is too large for your body and can hurt you.

7.4 Summary

- Every material substance (everything that is made of atoms) has electrons.

- Metals are called conductors.

- Electrons move from atom to atom in a conductor much like water moves through a garden hose.

- Other materials, like plastic, are called insulators. Electrons do not move through these.

Chapter 8   Magnets

8.1 Introduction

In Chapter 6 you learned that electrons have a negative charge and protons have a positive charge. Remember, this is just one way to say that the charges are opposite.

If you look around, you can see lots of different kinds of opposites. Black is the opposite of white. Wet is the opposite of dry. Dark is the opposite of light. North is the opposite of south. East is the opposite of west.

Sometimes opposites attract. In Chapter 6 you learned that positive charges attract negative charges. So, opposite charges will attract each other. This attraction creates the force that holds atoms together.

Some materials create attractive forces that aren't charged. A magnet is a type of material that will create an attractive force, but a magnet is not charged. Although a magnet is not charged, a magnet has opposite poles, and the opposite poles attract.

8.2 Magnetic Poles

All materials not only have electrons, but all the electrons are spinning. Magnets are usually made of nickel or iron. Some materials, like copper, don't make magnets. In metals that aren't magnetic, there are an equal number of electrons spinning. But in metals that are magnetic, like nickel or iron, there are an unequal number of electrons spinning. Because these metals have an unequal number of electrons spinning, they create magnetic poles.

One way to think about magnetic poles is to imagine a box full of marbles. Imagine that you have an equal number of marbles. Imagine also that each marble is half white and half black. To make it simple, imagine that you also gave all the marbles a "rule."

The rule is: "The marbles have to be balanced." So, for every marble with the black side facing forward, there must also be a marble with the black side facing backward. For every marble with the black side facing upward, there must be a marble with the black side facing downward. This way the black and white colors on the marbles are balanced.

If you throw all the marbles into the box, there will be a mixture of marbles. Some of the marbles will have the black side facing up; some will have the black side facing down.

Some marbles will have the black side facing forward and some backward. The marbles will be mixed, but because there is an equal number of marbles, all the directions the marbles are facing balance out.

Now imagine that you throw one more marble in the box. This marble has the black side facing up. But there isn't another marble to balance this one out. So what do the marbles do?

In a metal, this is what happens with the electrons. Because there is an extra electron on metal atoms, the spins are not balanced.

One way to get more balance is for all the marbles to line up in one direction. When the marbles do this, the effect of one extra marble is not so noticeable.

All the black sides face one way, and all the white sides face the other way. Since all the marbles are facing the same way, you could say that one side of the box is "white" and the other side is "black." In this way, the box has "opposite" sides.

In a metal, when the extra electron gets all the electrons spinning in the same direction, it is just like having all the marbles line up with the white sides pointing in one direction and the black sides pointing in the other direction. In a metal, this creates a magnetic pole.

Because the poles in a magnet are not charged, we don't call them "positive" and "negative." Instead we say "north" and "south." The north and south poles are opposite and attract each other.

Sometimes magnets will have the letters "N" and "S" written on them. These letters mean "North" and "South."

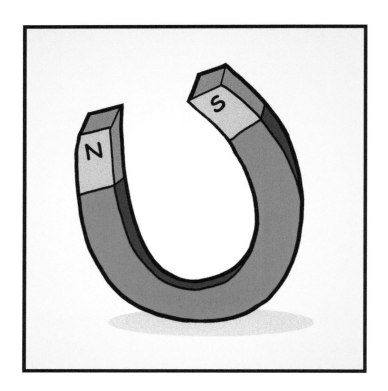

8.3 Magnets and Force

If you have played with magnets, you may have observed how one pole of a magnet will strongly attach to the opposite pole of another magnet. You also might have observed how the same poles of two magnets won't go together. No matter how hard you try to push them together, the same poles will not touch. If you hold the magnets in your hands, you can feel the force of the poles attracting each other or pushing each other away. This force is called a magnetic force.

Magnetic forces are caused by the spinning electrons inside magnetic metals. The forces generated by magnets can be quite strong. Magnets can be used to lift cars or hold heavy equipment together. The Earth is also a huge magnet! If you travel north anywhere on the Earth, you'll end up at the North Pole. If you travel south anywhere on the Earth you'll end up at the South Pole. The North and South Poles are the ends of the magnet we live on called Earth!

8.4 Summary

● A magnet has opposite poles.

● Only some metals, like nickel or iron, can be magnets.

● Magnetic force is caused by spinning electrons.

Chapter 9   Light and Sound

9.1 Waves

The next time you take a bath, notice the water. With the tub full and the water turned off, notice how the water is calm and smooth. Then place your foot in the tub and watch what the water does. If you observe carefully, you can probably see waves of water moving

away from your foot toward the sides of the tub and maybe even bouncing back.

Notice that if you put your foot into the tub slowly, you make small waves. If you put your foot into the tub quickly, you can make bigger waves. You can make small waves or big waves depending on how fast you make the water move. Notice also that the waves change over time.

If your dad puts his foot in quickly, the wave might be big and move fast. But, if you keep watching the water, you can see that the

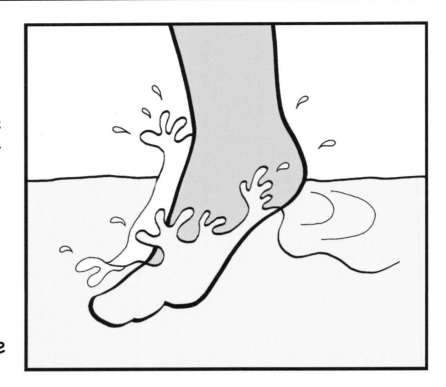

waves slow down and eventually disappear. Waves can be big or small, fast or slow.

If you look carefully at the wave, you might be

able to see that there is a high part and a low part to the wave. Scientists call the high part of a wave the peak, and the low part of the wave the valley.

9.2 Light Waves

It may not seem like it, but light behaves like water waves. It has "wave-like" characteristics, just like water. Light is actually a combination of electric waves and magnetic waves put together in a special way. Light is called an electromagnetic wave.

If you go outside during a sunny day, you see light coming from the Sun. You might think that

the Sun's light is "white" light, but really it is many colors of light put together. If you hold a prism in the sunlight, the prism separates the different colors of light. With a prism you can see all the colors that make sunlight. You see red, orange, yellow, green, blue, and violet.

The prism actually separates long, slow light waves (red) from short, fast light waves (blue). Both red and blue light are made of the same "light," but the length and speed of their waves are different, and that is why their colors are different.

Have you ever wondered why there is a rainbow in the sky when it is raining? The water droplets act like little prisms. The sunlight goes through the water droplets, and the water droplets separate the different waves of sunlight into different colors.

9.3 Sound Waves

Sound waves are also like water waves, except sound waves are waves of moving air molecules. If you clap your hands, what happens? You hear a sharp sound, and then it fades. Clap them again. You can again hear a sharp sound, and then the sound fades.

When you clap your hands, you are suddenly moving the air molecules near your hands. The air molecules move so much and so fast that they move all the way into your ear drums! And you hear a sound.

However, once the clap is over, the air molecules bounce around and then settle. This is why the sound fades. The air molecules move through the space around them as a wave. The sound wave rises and then falls, just like the water waves in the bathtub. Eventually the sound wave fades, just like the water wave fades, and this is why the sound goes away.

9.4 Summary

- A wave has a peak and a valley.

- A light wave is called an electromagnetic wave.

- Sunlight is made of different colors of light. Each color of light has a different wave.

- Sound is a wave of moving air molecules.

Chapter 10 Saving Energy

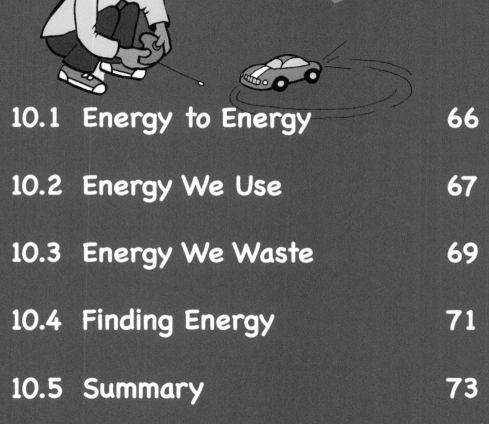

10.1 Energy to Energy

In this book you have learned about how energy is used when a force does work. You also learned about different kinds of energy. You learned about stored energy in batteries and cereal, and you also learned about moving energy. You learned about electrical energy and magnetic energy. You also saw energy in the form of light and sound. There are many different ways to describe energy and many different ways energy is used for forces and work.

If you look carefully at your brother when he is riding a bicycle, you can observe different types of energy being used to generate different kinds of forces and work.

Your brother's body is using chemical energy from his breakfast to move his muscles. The muscles are using the chemical energy to move the pedals on the bike. The pedals on the bike are connected to a chain and a gear. As the chain and the gear move, the wheels move. The chain, gear, and wheels are all using mechanical energy to move the bike forward.

In this example, you can see how one type of energy is getting converted, or changed, into another type of energy. Energy is only converted (or changed) into other types of energy. Energy is never created, and energy is never destroyed. It is only changed from one form to another.

10.2 Energy We Use

When your dad puts gas in the car, he is giving the car energy it can use. Your body can't use gasoline to move the pedals on a bicycle, but a car uses gasoline to run the motor. Likewise, a car cannot use cereal to move its motor like you use cereal to give energy to your legs.

There are different forms of energy, and not all types of energy can be used in the same way.

Gasoline is one form of energy that is used to power things like cars and boats. Cereal and bread are another form of energy used to power things like human bodies. Batteries are yet another form of energy used to power things like flashlights and laptop computers.

When we "use" energy, we are converting one form of energy to another form of energy.

When you use batteries in a music player, the chemical energy in the batteries is converted to moving and sound energy in the music player.

Eventually the batteries run out. All the chemical energy is converted to moving and sound energy, and there is no more chemical energy in the batteries. This is how we "use" energy. We convert it from one form to another form.

10.3 Energy We Waste

Even though energy cannot be destroyed, it is possible to "waste" energy. You might have heard your dad telling you to turn off the lights after you leave a room. Or you might hear your mom tell you not to leave the door open in the middle of winter. They may have told you not to "waste" energy. But if energy cannot be destroyed, what does it mean to waste energy?

Energy is "wasted" when energy is excessively or unnecessarily converted from one form to another form.

If you are playing with your battery powered car, then you are converting one form of energy (chemical energy in the battery) to another form of energy (moving energy in the car). Because you are playing with the car, it is necessary to convert the chemical energy.

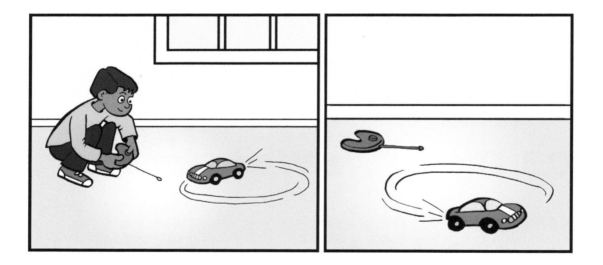

But if you walk away from the car, and you forget to turn it off, the battery is running but you are no longer playing with the car. Now you are "wasting" the energy in the battery because you are not using it to play with the car. When you go back to your car the next day, you discover it won't work anymore because the battery is "dead." All the chemical energy in the battery is gone. This is wasting energy. You didn't destroy the energy, you just unnecessarily converted it from chemical to moving energy when you didn't need to.

10.4 Finding Energy

We get much of our energy from the Earth. Gasoline, coal, and natural gas all come from inside the Earth. Nuclear energy also comes from the Earth in the form of plutonium. It is possible to get energy from moving water or wind, and we can also get energy from the Sun.

The food we eat comes from the Earth. We grow plants and raise animals to get food for our bodies. The plants get their energy from the Earth and also from the Sun.

Will we ever run out of energy? Yes and no. Energy from gasoline comes from fossils. There are only so many fossils in the ground, so it is possible that one day we will have used all the fossil energy. When that happens, there will not be any more gasoline coming from fossils to run our cars. This is also true with other forms of energy, such as coal or natural gas.

But if we remember that energy cannot be destroyed, only converted from one form to another, it may be possible to discover new ways to convert energy. Maybe there are new ways to convert the Sun's energy to chemical energy. Or maybe there are ways to get chemical energy from rocks. Or maybe there are ways to get electrical energy from grass or trees. Maybe you will be the next scientist who discovers a new way to convert energy into a form that can be used to power cars or boats or planes!

10.5 Summary

- Energy is neither created nor destroyed.

- Energy is converted from one form to another form.

- Energy is wasted by converting it from one form to another form excessively or unnecessarily.

- There may be new ways to convert energy to a form that can be used for fuel.

CPSIA information can be obtained
at www.ICGtesting.com
Printed in the USA
BVHW021406281118
533927BV00017BC/125/P